ONE NATION
Haitian Americans

Nichol Bryan

ABDO
Publishing Company

visit us at
www.abdopub.com

Published by ABDO Publishing Company, 4940 Viking Drive, Edina, Minnesota 55435.
Copyright © 2004 by Abdo Consulting Group, Inc. International copyrights reserved in all
countries. No part of this book may be reproduced in any form without written permission from
the publisher.

Printed in the United States.

Cover Photo: Corbis
Interior Photos: AP/Wide World pp. 16, 22; Corbis pp. 1, 2-3, 5, 6, 8, 9, 10, 13, 14, 19, 20, 21, 23,
    25, 26-27, 29, 30-31; TimePix p. 17

Editors: Kate A. Conley, Jennifer R. Krueger, Kristin Van Cleaf
Art Direction & Maps: Neil Klinepier

All of the U.S. population statistics in the One Nation series are taken from the 2000 Census.

Library of Congress Cataloging-in-Publication Data

Bryan, Nichol, 1958-
    Haitian Americans / Nichol Bryan.
        p. cm. -- (One nation)
    Summary: Provides an overview of the life and culture of Haitian Americans and presents
    some information on the history of Haiti.
    Includes bibliographical references (p.) and index.
    ISBN 1-57765-982-1
    1. Haitian Americans--Juvenile literature. [1. Haitian Americans. 2. Refugees. 3. Immigrants.]
I. Title.

E184.H27B78 2003
973'.049697294--dc21

                                                                        2002043632

Contents

Haitian Americans

Haiti is a land of beauty and color. It has a rich **culture**, mixing African and European languages and religions. But, Haiti is also a land of violence and poverty. Many of its people have been forced to flee for their lives. Like many other threatened people, they have turned to America for a home.

Every year, thousands of Haitians come to the United States, hoping to become American citizens. They join a nation made up of many different **immigrant** groups and their **descendants**. They share the hopes of earlier immigrants who came to America for safety, freedom, and opportunity.

Haitian Americans find that living in their new country has its challenges. Many face **discrimination** and other hardships as they try to learn a new language and fit into a new culture. They struggle to hold onto their past, while looking to their future in a new land. Some Haitian Americans long to return to their home country, while others doubt they ever will.

This Haitian-American girl lives in the Little Haiti section of Miami, Florida.

A Troubled Past

Haiti is a small country in the Caribbean Sea. It is located on the western end of an island called Hispaniola. The eastern part of Hispaniola is home to Haiti's neighbor, the Dominican Republic.

Christopher Columbus, an Italian explorer on a journey for Spain, landed on Hispaniola in 1492. Since his landing, the area has had a troubled history. The Spaniards made the native people slaves. Most of Hispaniola's native people died under this harsh treatment.

The French took control of the western end of Hispaniola in 1697. In the 1700s, the French brought African

A man brings in seashells to a beach in Haiti.

slaves to work on this land. These slaves eventually revolted, winning their freedom in 1804. They formed the country of Haiti.

Freedom, however, didn't solve all of Haiti's problems. For the next 200 years, governments and **dictators** struggled for power in Haiti. Then in 1915, the United States invaded Haiti in an effort to bring order to the country. The U.S. **occupation** lasted 19 years.

The Journey from Haiti to the United States

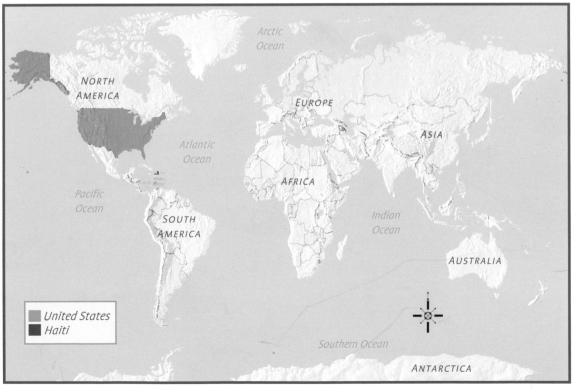

Haiti's troubles worsened when a man named François Duvalier was elected president in 1957. He was a cruel **dictator**. His son, who ruled after him, was also a dictator. The people of Haiti protested against Duvalier's son. He eventually fled the country in 1986. The next year, elections to choose a new president ended when the military violently took over the country.

François Duvalier reads a speech in 1957.

Elections were held again in 1990, and a man named Jean-Bertrand Aristide was elected president. The next year, the military regained control when soldiers threw Aristide out of the country. It seemed that Haiti's political problems would never end.

During this time, many Haitians tried to leave by boat. Many of them suffered or died on the voyage from their native land. The U.S. Coast Guard picked up about 35,000 Haitians in 1991 and 1992. Most were returned to Haiti. Despite this, **refugees** kept trying to reach the United States.

This girl lives in one of the poorest parts of Port-au-Prince, Haiti's capital.

In 1994, U.S. troops again went to Haiti to try to restore **democracy**. President Aristide was able to return. American forces tried to keep the peace. Then in 2000, Aristide was re-elected to head the government. Many Haitians protested. They believed the elections were **rigged** and that Aristide was becoming a **dictator**.

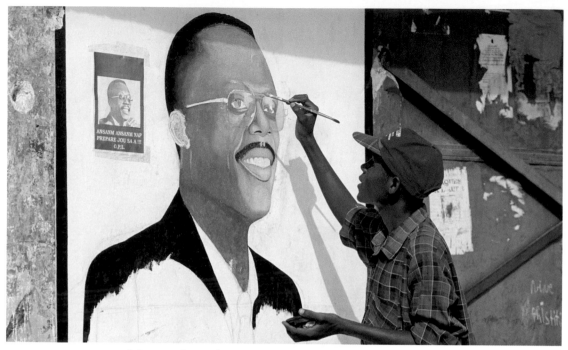

A Haitian artist paints a portrait of Jean-Bertrand Aristide.

Some people hoped that **democratic** elections would bring real change to Haiti. But, most of Haiti's 7 million people are still poor. Many Haitians work as farmers. Poor farming practices, however, have caused the soil to lose its fertility. This makes it even harder for Haitians to grow food and to make money. In fact, the average Haitian makes less than $400 a year.

Much of Haiti's land has been **deforested**. Today, less than 5 percent of Haiti is forested. That means people have little wood to burn for cooking and heat. There are few paved roads, and there are no working railroads.

Severe weather, such as **hurricanes** and **droughts**, also makes life difficult for Haitians. In 1998, Hurricane Georges struck the island. More than 400 people died, and thousands lost their homes. Though international groups tried to help, conditions were terrible. More boats filled with **refugees** left the island.

With all these problems, some Haitian leaders hope that foreigners will support the island with money. But, because of government **corruption** and the flood of refugees, many people are afraid to invest in Haiti. With little hope for their country, Haitians continue to leave for the United States.

Voyage to America

Some Haitians are so desperate to find a better life that they risk everything to get away. Many have died in unsafe boats on the ocean voyage to the United States. These **refugees** often pay all the money they have to board a boat that is not even fit to sail. And, dishonest sea captains pack the boats with too many people.

Even if the boats don't sink, there are other dangers. There is often little or no food or fresh water. There are no toilets or showers, and disease may spread in the crowded boats. With conditions such as these, the boat trip can kill the young and the weak.

The voyage is dangerous for other reasons, too. Haitian boats do not always have navigational equipment. The craft can get lost and sail out into the ocean, far from any land. Other ships do not always stop to help sinking or lost boats. And when a storm hits, a boat filled with refugees can flip over.

Opposite page: These Haitian refugees
hope to reach the shores of Florida.

In spite of the dangers, people keep coming to the United States from Haiti. About 181,000 Haitians came to America between 1989 and 2000. Some are allowed to stay. But, most Haitian **refugees** are sent back because of U.S. **immigration** policies. They return to Haiti to face a hard future.

Settling In

Most Haitian Americans live along the East Coast of the United States. Many live as far north as Boston, Massachusetts. Almost half a million Haitians live in and around New York, New York. Another large group of Haitian Americans lives in Miami, Florida.

Haitian immigrants who are picked up by the U.S. Coast Guard face an uncertain future.

Some of the first Haitians to arrive in America landed on a wealthy beachfront area in Florida. The residents there set up a kitchen on the beach to feed the **immigrants**. Along with this welcoming, however, Haitian immigrants have also dealt with **discrimination** and other challenges.

Fortunately, many organizations have helped Haitians adjust to life in their new country. Haitians are now one of the fastest-growing **ethnic** groups in the eastern United States. But, the government continues to turn away hundreds of Haitians trying to reach America by sea.

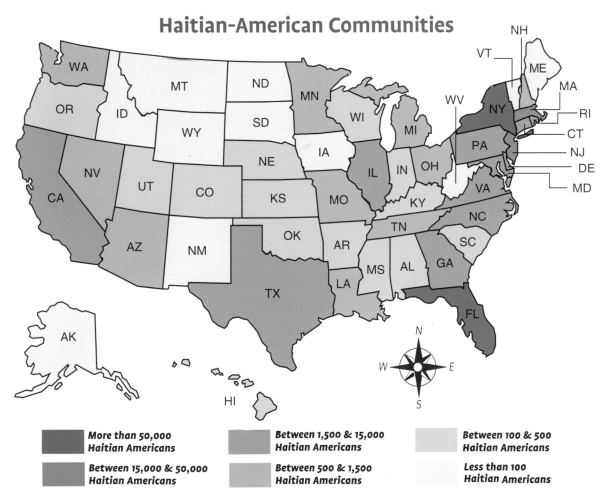

Haitian-American Communities

More than 50,000 Haitian Americans

Between 15,000 & 50,000 Haitian Americans

Between 1,500 & 15,000 Haitian Americans

Between 500 & 1,500 Haitian Americans

Between 100 & 500 Haitian Americans

Less than 100 Haitian Americans

A young Haitian American attends a naturalization ceremony.

Those who are lucky enough to stay in the United States still have a tough life ahead of them. Half of all Haitians cannot read. Therefore, many must learn to read at the same time they learn English. Because Haitian-American children learn English at school, they sometimes speak better English than their parents!

Not knowing English makes it hard for some Haitians to get jobs. One of the largest Haitian populations is in Florida, where many of these **immigrants** work in low-paying jobs while they learn English. But, there are also Haitian doctors, lawyers, and professors in the

United States. Some Haitian Americans own their own businesses or have succeeded in politics.

The most fortunate Haitians are those with family members already in the United States. Families can support new arrivals. And families can help new **immigrants** find work as they try to become citizens.

Haitian Americans have built a close community as they help each other. For example, several U.S. radio stations report on Haitian activities. Many people in the United States and Haiti read a weekly newspaper called the *Haitian Times*. Its award-winning writers and photographers report on Haiti as well as Haitian-American issues.

*Haitian immigrants studying
English in Little Haiti*

Becoming a Citizen

Haitians and other **immigrants** who come to the United States take the same path to citizenship. Immigrants become citizens in a process called naturalization. A government agency called the Immigration and Naturalization Service (INS) oversees this process.

The Path to Citizenship

Applying for Citizenship

The first step in becoming a citizen is filling out a form. It is called the Application for Naturalization. On the application, immigrants provide information about their past. Immigrants send the application to the INS.

Providing Information

Besides the application, immigrants must provide the INS with other items. They may include documents such as marriage licenses or old tax returns. Immigrants must also provide photographs and fingerprints. They are used for identification. The fingerprints are also used to check whether immigrants have committed crimes in the past.

The Interview

Next, an INS officer interviews each immigrant to discuss his or her application and background. In addition, the INS officer tests the immigrant's ability to speak, read, and write in English. The officer also tests the immigrant's knowledge of American civics.

The Oath

Immigrants approved for citizenship must take the Oath of Allegiance. Once immigrants take this oath, they are citizens. During the oath, immigrants promise to renounce loyalty to their native country, to support the U.S. Constitution, and to serve and defend the United States when needed.

Sample Questions from the Civics Test

How many stars are there on our flag?

What is the capital of the state you live in?

Why did the pilgrims come to America?

How many senators are there in Congress?

Who said, "Give me liberty or give me death"?

What are the first 10 amendments to the Constitution called?

In what month do we vote for the president?

Why Become a Citizen?

Why would an immigrant want to become a U.S. citizen? There are many reasons. Perhaps the biggest reason is that the U.S. Constitution grants many rights to its citizens. One of the most important is the right to vote.

U.S. Department of Justice
Immigration and Naturalization Service

Print clearly or type your answers using CAPITAL letters. Failure to print clearly may delay your application. Use bl

Application f

Part 1. Your Name *(The Person Applying for Naturalization)*

A. Your current legal name.

Family Name *(Last Name)*

Write your INS "A"- n

A _ _ _ _ _ _

Given Name *(First Name)*

Full Middle Name *(If applicable)*

FOR INS US

Bar Code

B. Your name exactly as it appears on your Permanent Resident Card.

Family Name *(Last Name)*

Given Name *(First Name)*

Full Middle Name *(If applicable)*

C. If you have ever used other names, provide them below.

Family Name *(Last Name)*

Given Name *(First Name)*

Middle Name

Haitian Heritage

Haitian **culture** mixes French and Roman Catholic traditions with African **customs**. Haitian Americans have brought this rich culture with them to their new home. The customs of Haitian Americans can be seen in their families and music, as well as in their food, language, and religion.

Family

Haitian families often make important decisions in a family council. This council is made up of the most important family members, including grandparents. When grandparents are too old to live by themselves, they often move in with their adult children.

A Haitian-American family

Most Haitian-American families are very close. Often, everyone works hard to earn money. Children who are old enough may work to help support their family. This can make it hard for them to go to after-school activities, because they must spend their time working at part-time jobs.

A waitress at Tap Tap, a famous Haitian restaurant in Florida

Haitian Americans perform a traditional dance in Miami.

Music

   Many Haitian Americans love American music, but they also listen to island music called *konpa*. *Konpa* is Haiti's national dance music. It mixes Latin music, American soul and rock, and drumming inspired by Haitian voodoo ceremonies.

Food

Food is another important part of Haitian **culture**. Like much of its culture, Haiti's food has been influenced by African and European traditions. Haitian Americans like foods that are spicy. They also eat a lot of rice and beans. Popular meats in Haiti include fish, goat, and chicken. Many Haitian Americans eat these foods in the United States.

Language

French and Haitian Creole are the official languages of Haiti. Many Haitian Americans speak Haitian Creole at home. Haitian Creole is based on French. It also has some Spanish and African words. Communicating can be difficult for Haitian Americans who don't know English. That's because most other Americans speak neither French nor Haitian Creole.

A marketplace in Little Haiti

Body Language

Haitians communicate by more than just spoken language. They also use body language that may be unfamiliar to other Americans. For example, a Haitian-American student may not look a teacher in the eye as a sign of respect. Haitian Americans may also talk loudly and stand close to each other, even when they are not arguing. And, Haitian children often greet people with a kiss on the cheek.

Religion

Haitians honor many religious traditions. Roughly four of every five Haitians are members of the Roman Catholic Church. Many others are Protestant. These Christian religions were brought to Haiti by Spanish and French rulers, and the United States.

However, half of all Haitians, including Catholics, also follow voodoo. This religion is a mix of African and Christian beliefs. Voodoo includes medicine, justice, dance, and music.

Voodoo has been around since the French brought African slaves to Haiti. Although followers of voodoo believe in one god, many spirits are also a part of voodoo. Followers believe that spirits constantly affect the lives of living people.

Many Haitian Americans have Roman Catholic symbols in their homes. But, some may not openly show signs of following voodoo. That is because they feel voodoo is misunderstood in the United States.

A woman reads a prayer book in a Catholic center in Little Haiti.

Giving Back

Haitian Americans contribute to all parts of American society, including government. In 2000, Philip Brutus became the first Haitian American elected to Florida's state government. He represents many people, including those who live in Little Haiti. Little Haiti is a large community of Haitian Americans in Florida.

Another notable part of Haitian-American **culture** is **visual** art. Paintings that use bright colors to capture a scene are very popular. But, Haitian art has also developed into many different styles.

A woman displays typical Haitian art.

Since the 1940s, American collectors have been interested in the work of self-taught Haitian artists. Some Haitian-American and Haitian artists paint their homeland as a green and sunny place. Other artists concentrate on the challenges facing Haiti.

Perhaps the most famous Haitian-American artist was Jean-Michel Basquiat. Basquiat was born in Brooklyn, New York, but his father came from Haiti. Basquiat sold hand-painted postcards and T-shirts to make money. He was soon discovered by the art world. He became one of America's most important young artists before his death in 1988.

Haitian Americans have also succeeded as writers. Edwidge Danticat is a talented Haitian-American writer. The author of several books, she has also taught at the University of Miami. Danticat was nominated for a National Book Award for her book *Krik? Krak!*, a short story collection about Haitians and Haitian Americans.

Like Danticat, author Dany Laferrière also lives in Miami. He has written a dozen novels. Most were originally published in French, but many have been translated into English. Laferrière's books include *An Aroma of Coffee* and *Dining with the Dictator*.

Opposite page: Jean-Michel Basquiat displays his art.

Many Haitian Americans contribute to American society while thinking about returning to Haiti someday. In the meantime, the **culture** of Haiti flourishes in Haitian-American communities around the United States.

Glossary

corrupt - showing dishonest or improper behavior.

culture - the customs, arts, and tools of a nation or people at a certain time.

customs - the habits of a group that are passed on through generations.

deforested - cleared of forests or trees.

democracy - a governmental system in which the people vote on how to run their country.

descendant - a person who comes from a particular ancestor or group of ancestors.

dictator - a ruler with complete control who usually governs in an unfair way.

discrimination - unfair treatment based on factors such as a person's race, religion, or gender.

drought - a long period of dry weather.

ethnic - of or having to do with a group of people who have the same race, nationality, or culture.

hurricane - a tropical storm with strong circular winds, rain, thunder, and lightning.

immigration - entry into another country to live. People who immigrate are called immigrants.

occupation - the owning or controlling of a certain area.

refugee - a person who flees to another country for safety and protection.

rigged - set up or controlled in an unfair way.

visual - able to be seen.

Saying It

Dany Laferrière - DON-ee LA-fee-air
Edwidge Danticat - ed-WEEDJ dan-tih-KAH
François Duvalier - frah-SWAH dooh-VAL-yay
Hispaniola - his-puhn-YOH-luh
Jean-Bertrand Aristide - zhah-bur-TRAND air-ih-STEED
Jean-Michel Basquiat - zhah-mee-SHEL bahs-kee-AHT
konpa - KOHN-pah

Web Sites

To learn more about Haitian Americans, visit ABDO Publishing
Company on the World Wide Web at **www.abdopub.com**. Web
sites about Haitian Americans are featured on our Book Links page.
These links are routinely monitored and updated to provide the
most current information available.

31

Index